CoolBrands® 2021/22

An insight into some of Britain's coolest brands

Credits

CoolBrands.uk.com   2021/2022

Damon Segal

Chief Executive

Nathan Mathan

Director

Felisa Kennard

Chief Operating Officer

Ed Dawes

Brand Liaison Director

Charlotte Posner

Cover Artist

Veronica Nobili

Design Director

Published by **Academy of Chief Marketers**

William Old Centre Duck's Hill Rd
Northwood HA6 2NP

Paper supplied by Sappi

Printed in the UK by Geoff Neal Group

ISBN: 978-1-8382519-2-5

Foreword

written by

Damon Segal & Nathan Mathan

The word cool is almost everywhere, from magazines, books, commercials and in marketing. Even though the origins of this word and its relation to branding have long been discussed, there hasn't been much scientific study of coolness and its effects on brand quality and brand loyalty. However, while cool is an elusive and intangible concept, being cool almost always means increased financial profits with high ticket pricing, insatiable consumer demand, and clever image enhancement beyond your control. It can even be a significant barrier to competing brands.

Why is it cool to be cool? I find that question one that pops up in conversation quite a lot.

Cool branding has become very important in the last few years, with many big brand names like Tesla, Spotify and Peloton standing out for their coolness last year, and many smaller companies starting to catch on like Wild, Veja and Craig Green.

We know that cool conveys a certain attitude, a notion of non-conformity, with generations now less concerned with social stigmas. Many brands fear being left behind in the modern digital marketplace, especially as the rapid adoption of social media and smartphones continues to influence consumer buying behaviour.

Whether they are young or established, many brands understand that they must be relevant, interesting, or cutting-edge to survive. However, this perspective ignores the importance of being cool and making deeper connections with consumers on the ground floor.

Cool is a marketing concept that has emerged as a management strategy over time. It evolved out of traditional branding, which aimed to make brands more memorable and relevant. The emerging framework of cool focuses on creating credibility, excitement, and authenticity centred around the core values for brands in the digital age.

When a brand makes its way into the consciousness of consumers, it achieves what branding is all about: the extraordinary quality where consumers perceive a difference between what they see and what they get, compared to competitor brands. This difference inspires consumers to take action. Brands need to be distinctive, exciting, or even mysterious to stand out in a noisy digital and consumer arena. Unique content is one of the most important aspects of being considered cool. By creating new and unique content, a brand can show an innovative vision and that it is not afraid to be different.

We understand that the meaning behind being cool is more complex than a simple rating on a scale. On one end, coolness may be related to a customers' fear of being left out by those who support a given brand. On the other hand, coolness can also be related to a brand's ability to create a buzz through successful ad or marketing campaigns that are cool and unusual enough to make people talk about it. Whatever the meaning behind being cool, one thing is certain: if you want to stand out in your industry, it helps to have cool values and communicate what makes your brand different in your advertising and marketing campaigns.

We want to thank all those on our expert council for their generous time to help us establish this year's CoolBrands results.

The CoolBrands annual is a celebration of some of the brand stories of those who achieved the status of CoolBrand 2021/22. We hope you enjoy reading it as much as we did putting it together.

Contents

About
CoolBrands®

CoolBrands® is an annual initiative to identify and pay tribute to the nation's coolest brands.

Since 2001 we have been canvassing the opinions of experts and consumers to produce an annual barometer of Britain's coolest brands.

Cool is subjective and personal. Accordingly, voters are not given a definition but are asked to bear in mind the following factors, which research has shown are inherent in all CoolBrands®...

Authenticity
Desirability
Innovation
Originality
Responsibility

*Brands do not apply or pay to be considered for CoolBrands® status.

Who chooses the CoolBrands®?

The 2021/22 Expert Council

The 2021/22 CoolBrands® were chosen by an Expert Council. The entire selection process is independently administered by The Centre for Brand Analysis – visit CoolBrands.uk.com for full details.

James Balfour
Co-founder, 1Rebel

Tim Beaumont
Founder, Beaumont London

John Booth
Artist

Edith Bowman
DJ, radio presenter & television personality

Charlie Casley-Hayford
Menswear designer and co-founder

Dominic Cools-Lartigue
Founder, Street Feast

Josh Cuthbert
Model & Creative

DJ Spoony
DJ, Radio presenter & television personality

Erin Doherty
Actor

Nicola Fontanella
Founder, Argent Design

Michael Fox
Actor

Glyn Fussell
Co-creator of Sink the Pink & Presenter

David Gandy
Model

Maria Hatzistefanis
Founder, RODIAL

Katie Hillier
Creative director & accessories designer

Henry Holland
Designer

Tom Honeyands
The Tech Chap

Seema Jaswal
Sports presenter & event host

David Jonsson
Actor

Chanté Joseph
Writer & broadcaster

Leyla Kazim
Broadcaster & presenter

Roman Kemp
Radio host & broadcaster

Millie Kendall
CEO, British Beauty Council

Ferdinand Kingsley
Actor

Mark Krendel
Founder, 8lbs

Caspar Lee
YouTuber & entrepreneur

SG Lewis
Singer-songwriter, musician & record producer

Hannah Marshall
Creative director & multi-disciplinary artist

Liz Matthews
Entertainment publicist

Zara McDermott
Model & influencer

Natalie Melton
Creative director, The Craft Council

Nachson Mimran
Founder To.org & Together Band

Mr JWW
Co-founder of @theproductionbunker

Brenock O'Connor
Actor

Dermot O'Leary
Presenter & radio DJ

Melissa Odabash
Fashion designer

Michelle Ogundehin
Writer, consultant & TV presenter

Caroline Rush
CEO, British Fashion Council

Juliet Sear
TV baker & author

Niomi Smart
Wellness & lifestyle blogger

James Stewart
Heart Radio host

The Thinking Drinkers
Drinks writers & comedy performers

John Vial
Celebrity hairdresser & founder, Sloane Salon

Harriet Vine
MBE creative director & co-founder, Tatty Devine

Stephen Webster
British jewellery designer

Sian Welby
TV & radio presenter

Lucy Williams
Digital creative & consultant

Steven Wilson
Artist

Bonnie Wright
Actress, film-maker & activist

How do brands evolve and continue to be cool?

Some brands are timeless as generation after generation falls in love with them.

Think of brands like Apple, Nike, and Beyonce, and you will see that they have stood the test of time. One of the reasons why they continue to find new audiences is because people believe they are cool.

Coolness is one of those concepts that's hard to define, and it's also a trait that most brands would love to have. Marketers spend hundreds of millions of dollars every year in hopes that their brands will become cool. But few manage to achieve it.

It's not just companies that are actively pursuing this. Politicians, sports teams, and even countries want to be perceived as cool.

The belief seems that if you are cool, it will be easier to find acceptance and allegiance. In a market saturated with products with little differentiation, its coolness will help a brand prevail, or so the thinking goes.

Which begs the question, what exactly is cool? Is there a way to define it that makes it easy to assess the success of those brands regarded as cool?

Defining cool

Cool can be defined as being unique, original, relevant, and with a non-conformist attitude. That doesn't mean it's all about rebellion, and it means that cool is a state of thinking beyond the obvious and not easily accepting the received ideas.

What makes a brand cool

The Journal of Marketing did a study to analyse coolness in depth. The authors found out that when a brand is cool, it will embody these ten characteristics:

Extraordinary

The brand would deliver demonstrable and superior-quality benefits.

Aesthetically appealing

It would be desirable and a trendsetter for its category and the industry.

Energetic

It would also be perceived as outgoing and active, helping people have exceptional experiences.

High status

The brand would be stylish, exclusive, refined, and sophisticated.

Rebellious

It wouldn't accept the existing codes and strive to break the rules, be irreverent, and be rebellious.

Original

A cool brand would be unlike anything in its category, and it would be imaginative and creative and redefine the space it operates in.

Authentic

It would be true to its roots and wouldn't mimic someone else's voice, tone, or manner.

Subcultural

It would be accepted and endorsed by a smaller group of people at first.

Iconic

The brand would have a unique meaning and value among its user base.

Popular

It would also be accepted by consumers and regarded as the trendsetter.

What doesn't guarantee coolness

Cool isn't category-specific. When marketers began to study the popularity and coolness factor of specific brands, an underlying assumption was that the category would be a dominant factor. But that hasn't turned out to be the case.

Just because a brand has a universally acknowledged cool brand doesn't mean its competitors or new entrants will automatically get that status.

For example, while Nike and Adidas are perceived to be cool, Reebok didn't come across the same attributes in the study mentioned above. Similarly, Apple is considered among the coolest brands on the planet, but its strongest competitor in software, Microsoft, is anything but cool.

Mere advertising doesn't do the trick. While it takes a well-crafted brand management strategy to make a brand cool, marketing alone won't give it its coolness. It depends more on the traits mentioned above and goes beyond the peripheral messages conveyed through advertising.

Those characteristics, along with user experience, will determine whether consumers think of a brand as cool. When it becomes cool, there will be significant word-of-mouth promotion for the brand.

Higher awareness won't translate to coolness. Just because a brand is well-known won't make it aspirational. Some of the most popular brands are not necessarily cool, while others with lesser visibility - and ad spends - may be perceived as cool.

LinkedIn, while highly popular, is nowhere as cool as Instagram. Everyone knows what Zoom is, but Skype has the coolness factor.

Cool isn't inherited. What may have been highly irresistible to a generation may not be relevant or valuable to the next. This is one of the greatest mysteries - and questions - in the study of coolness. The brand's cutting-edge appeal and creativity may have answered the needs of a particular time but may naturally come across as dated to another generation.

Volkswagen was one of the symbols of the cool, counterculture narrative of the 60s. Levis was denim for millions of youngsters in the 80s and 90s. United Colors of Benetton was edgy for a generation. But these brands stopped being cool for the following sets of consumers.

The stages of cool

Brands don't become cool overnight or stay that way perpetually. Most brands go through a path that takes them across three stages of "progressive coolness."

These transitions are influenced by the growth of its audience and societal factors that are outside its control.

What's important to understand is that this movement may or may not be intentionally designed. Some companies may initiate it, which will lead to the brand's growth and expansion of its product portfolio.

In other instances, brand management may have little to do with it, as consumers may decide when a brand crosses over to the next stage.

Whether marketers consciously steer the ship or whether consumer preferences are at play, it's good to know what stage a brand is at.

Stage 1 — Cool for some

At this stage, the brand isn't known to everyone in the market, and it's like a nightclub that only a select few know of. Those audiences, however, are staunch believers in the brand, and they have experienced it and identify as the elite with exclusive access to the brand.

The company, at this stage, may not be advertising the brand through any effective medium, and most traffic would be through word-of-mouth endorsement. Those early adopters will also profess to be experts on the brand and its uniqueness in the category. They will publicise the brand, favourably compare it to its competitors, and defend it from criticism.

In some cases, brands may not leave this limited-audience space. This frequently happens to products in the fashion and lifestyle categories. But cool brands in the digital space that can quickly scale will outgrow this phase. That's because it's exceedingly easy to add new users without having to replicate the product.

At this stage, the allure of the brand is predominantly because of its exclusivity. The brand is cool because not many know of it or use it other than the subculture of its customers.

Advantages of stage 1

Loyal customers: Although they may be a minority, the first set of consumers will be ardent believers and proponents of the brand. What makes it noteworthy is that their brand loyalty would be created without any mass communication from the brand.

Before it went mainstream, the trading app Robinhood had its faithful users who saw the brand as a counter-narrative to the prevalent trading options.

High level of admiration: The first set of users would have extraordinary levels of love for the brand. In many cases, they might interact with the brand owners and share their appreciation and feedback. These endorsements from users will be specific, making them credible and trustworthy for others.

Starlink is an excellent example of how a group of devout followers can profess their admiration online and get others interested in using the product.

Disadvantages of stage 1

Low brand awareness: Exclusivity also means limited attention, and not many outside the initial user base would be aware of the product.

Less revenue generation: A smaller set of consumers translates to lower levels of revenue for the brand. Although the brand may be cool for its users, there will be an upper cap on its income from these customers

Stage 2 — Cool for all

This is when brands move on from the initial niche cool to be cool for the mass market. Most brands would make the journey, but some could be still confined to a smaller set of users.

Those who do become cool for everyone will have a larger audience, encouraging them to expand their product portfolio.

As the brand becomes big, its identity and defining characteristics may dilute to cater to the larger market. Most brands at this stage will start losing their coolness as their identity becomes tied to the lowest common denominator of consumer preferences.

This might force the initial adopters to leave the brand as it may have become "too mainstream" for them.

What was once their exclusive experience has suddenly become commoditised for everyone. Several reports have suggested that Facebook, for example, could be at this stage where the initial set of users are leaving the platform.

This exodus will be non-negotiable and inevitable for most brands. It's also important to note that once the ardent followers leave, they are doubtful to return to the brand fold. But brand managers will now have a larger audience to cater to.

Advantages of stage 2

Higher brand awareness: When it crosses the tipping point from niche to mass, the brand will develop a more extensive set of consumers. Everyone knows the brand now due to heavy advertising and public relations. People who didn't have access earlier would want to experience the brand directly.

Higher revenue: With more users, the brand will generate higher revenue. This will help the brand managers spend more on advertising, further increasing brand recognition and revenue.

It will also encourage marketers to expand the product line and develop new variants for the mass market at different price tiers.

Disadvantages of stage 2

Loss of exclusivity: There's little exclusivity to the brand experience for consumers, which will discourage them from using or endorsing the product. This frequently happens in fashion as brands become "too common" or "mass market."

Marketers find a way out by launching premium extensions of the brand, which will still connote exclusivity.

iPhones will have both higher and slightly affordable price brackets, for example.

A slower rate of adoption: put simply, fewer people would find it cool now. Even if the brand was once the gold standard for the industry and was synonymous with the category, there will be fewer new consumers with everyone using it. Levi's found it out the hard way.

Stage 3 — Cool for none

By now, the brand has ceased to be cool for most consumers, and it isn't perceived as edgy, rebellious, aspirational, unique, or original.

This doesn't mean that the brand has died, been discontinued, or isn't generating revenue or profits.

What it means is that it's become a commodity. Those who use it won't flaunt it or endorse it openly. The reason people may prefer it might be due to its price advantage or ease of availability.

The brand will still be profitable, but it will be challenging to acquire new users based on brand attributes. Companies may have to indulge in other tactics, including discounts and bundled offers to stay relevant. Old Navy and MTV are two examples of brands that were once perceived as cool but are no longer edgy or original.

How to make a brand cool and relevant

Coolness is an irrational benefit of a brand that even its early adopters can't easily define. It takes exceptional creativity, consistency, and courage to make a brand cool and aspirational. While the given characteristics are what eventually get associated with coolness, no proven method will guarantee it.

But marketers can keep some best practices in mind to make a brand original and edgy. Analyses of most cool brands show that these should start from the moment a brand is conceived and not at the launch or relaunch stage.

Be original in design

The correct brand identity will go a long way in helping it appear cool to consumers. The brand name, logo, design, colour scheme, and tagline, along with its packaging, will help define its identity to potential users. Marketers should aim to make it as unique as possible.

If the brand character is "irreverent," the identity should capture it without the company explaining it in its marketing. If it's "bold," customers should easily understand the attribute. Beats by Dre is an excellent example of how to get it right, from the logo to the colour scheme to its packaging.

So, why doesn't it happen more often? Because brand managers' first instinct is to honour the category codes, making it easy for consumers to associate the brand with the category. But being original, imaginative, and even subverting category codes will pay rich dividends.

Bandages are one of the most uncool categories for consumers. Brands resemble each other, and there's little in terms of product differentiation. That is until Welly came out with their unique designs that broke all conventions.

Think beyond the present

Nobody was asking for 1000 songs in their pockets when Apple launched iPods. There wasn't a well-defined need-gap in the industry that the tech giant was addressing. They weren't trying to solve today's problems, and they were creating tomorrow's solutions.

This means that coolness needs to be thought of at the product development stage itself. While illusory brand attributes can be added later, differentiation at the product level will make the brand unique and cool.

Other than the demonstrable benefits, consumers prefer innovative firms because of the immediate elevation in their experiences. No other digital or non-digital brand could compete with iPod because it elevated consumer experiences way beyond the category benefits.

The second reason is that it puts a considerable distance between adopters and non-users which helps brands command a premium. People are willing to pay more for Apple products because they believe that its products are innovative and cooler than its competitors.

Thirdly, it invites customers into a cool ecosystem of future upgrades and brand extensions. Once people taste a cutting-edge product, they wouldn't want to trade that experience or downgrade it for price differences.

Engage with customers

If you want to create a subculture, you should know its participants. Most marketers are aware of understanding their customers, but their engagement becomes transactional and perfunctory. Cool brands don't talk to their customers for any specific motive, and they try to understand their users' lives, pain points, and aspirations.

Focus groups can never deliver an in-depth understanding of a brand's potential users. For that, marketers need to engage in long-term conversations and holistic studies of user groups. Ordinary research will give rise to everyday insights and solutions.

This has enormous implications for a brand's social media presence. Instead of making it a one-way lane, brand managers should listen to what customers would like to have in the brand, what tweaks they want, and what issues they usually face.

It's also an opportunity to share your weaknesses and failures. This goes against the conventional wisdom of sharing product features and offers. Nothing makes a brand appear relatable than its occasional missteps and the candid admissions of those.

Elon Musk doesn't just talk about Tesla's successes to his millions of followers, and he routinely shares the brand's failures and what they are learning from them. That sets him and the brand apart from the condescending tone of others.

Take a bold stance whenever needed

No brand operates in a vacuum. It's a product of the demands and challenges of the societies it caters to. More importantly, its customers don't evaluate brands as separate from the prevailing socioeconomic discourses. Cool brands know this and are not afraid to take a bold stance on issues that matter to their customers.

But it's easier said than done. Most marketers skirt the issue altogether because they don't want to alienate their existing users. So, confirmation seems the safe strategy, although it has long-term implications for brand loyalty and adoption.

Plus, it makes it easier for a challenger brand to defy the convention.

Nike explicitly supported Black Lives Matter when it was convenient for other brands to remain silent - or wait for someone else to take the lead. The brand boldly made Colin Kaepernick the face of its campaign. While several people went to the extent of burning Nike products, the company's sales increased by 31 per cent.

Patagonia celebrates the mountain runner Felipe Cancino's run through the Maipo River Valley in Chile to demonstrate the need to save that fragile ecosystem. These "runs to activism" are central to the brand's beliefs and its customers have entirely accepted and endorsed Patagonia's commitment to an adventurous lifestyle that values sustainability.

In short:

Being cool shouldn't be a short-term marketing objective, and it should be a long-term strategic goal that involves all stakeholders.

Eventually, it's about understanding the customers and developing an edgy, imaginative, socially relevant, and unconventional identity. Once a brand becomes cool, marketers need to understand what makes it tick and not dilute its coolness by spreading it too thin. Overdoing it by appealing to everyone can make a brand seem familiar.

Brand managers should always be on the lookout for the inflexion point when a previously cool brand resembles the ancestral voices in the category. That should be the clearest sign that the brand is losing its coolness.

1Rebel

1REBEL

King of gyms

Since 2015 1Rebel has been on a mission to disrupt the fitness industry.

London's top boutique fitness operator with five high-intensity class types; it's renowned for its global award-winning design, and unrelenting pursuit of exceptional customer experience, innovation and inspiration.

1Rebel led the movement away from single-use plastic in the fitness industry, with its "Rebel Against Plastic" campaign.

With 9 studios across London and over 60 top of their game trainers, plus studios in Australia and across the Middle East, 1Rebel is leading the way in the premium fitness space.

1rebel.com

Aromatherapy Associates

AROMATHERAPY
ASSOCIATES
LONDON

A world-leading wellbeing brand, specialising in essential oil blends

Aromatherapy Associates was founded in 1985, at the very beginning of modern aromatherapy movement.

Guided by its vision to offer accessible well-being to all, Aromatherapy Associates produces essential oil blends that help to reduce stress, boost energy and aid a better night's sleep.

Aromatherapy Associates proudly joined the global B Corporation movement in 2020, an important moment in the company's history confirming its pledge to put people and the planet on the same footing as profit.

'It's not just about being best in the world: it's about being best for the world.'
- Anna Teal, CEO

aromatherapyassociates.com

Beyond Meat

BEYOND MEAT®

#GoBeyond

The positive choices that we can make have a great impact.

We believe there is a better way to feed our future and that the positive choices we all make, no matter how small, can have a great impact on the health of our planet. By shifting from animal to plant-based meat, we can positively impact the growing global issues of climate change, constraints on natural resources, and animal welfare. We create delicious products that enable you to eat what you love without compromising on taste, sustainability, or a balanced lifestyle.

beyondmeat.com

Camp Bestival

We Are Family!

Camp Bestival combines an all-encompassing family festival experience with an action-packed camping holiday to create a Festi-Holiday!

The brainchild of renowned music specialist Rob da Bank and creative director Josie da Bank, Camp Bestival is known as the UK's ultimate family festival.

Taking place at the start of the summer holidays at Lulworth Castle on Dorset's stunning Jurassic Coast, Camp Bestival offers hundreds of things for families to do from circus skills, science explorations, bushcraft and immersive theatre journeys through to amazing live acts and DJs, family raves, comedy, cocktails, award-winning street food, and flamboyant evening cabaret, all shared with likeminded people.

campbestival.net

CAMPARI

CAMPARI

CAMPARI, the iconic, unforgettable Italian red spirit sitting at the heart of some of the world's most famous cocktails.

CAMPARI was founded in Milan in 1860 by Gaspare Campari, and pioneered by his son, Davide, who created something so distinctive and revolutionary that its secret recipe has not been altered since.

Vibrant red in colour, CAMPARI's unique and multi-layered taste is the result of the infusion of herbs, aromatic plants and fruit in alcohol and water.

As well as being unique and distinctive, CAMPARI is extremely versatile, offering boundless and unexpected possibilities.

As a source of this passionate inspiration since its creation seen through its founders' creative genius, artists in different fields and the world's best bartenders, CAMPARI stimulates your instincts to unlock your passions, inspiring limitless creations.

Discover your Red Passion

CAMPARI
RED PASSION

Red Passion

The Red Passion campaign is the latest in a long-standing series of unique, creative collaborations as CAMPARI partners with ground-breaking artists, spanning creative expression across a variety of fields.

Since its birth, CAMPARI has been a source of passionate inspiration, thanks to a history as rich and deep as the liquid itself, seen through its founders' creative genius.

CAMPARI has not only inspired passion in bartenders across the world to create iconic masterpieces at the forefront of cocktail culture, such as the Negroni and CAMPARI G&T but also through art and creativity, inspiring artists and filmmakers alike.

CAMPARI's visionary and forward-thinking attitude has constantly pushed the boundaries of creativity to go beyond the norm, exploring uncharted languages of advertising and tapping into the talent of artists, painters and designers.

The brand's deep-rooted affiliation with the creative world has seen limitless creations with world-famous names such as Fellini and Sorrentino to name a few, to visually express CAMPARI's passion and creativity in an intriguingly evocative way.

campari.com

CanO Water

CANO WATER®

The first ever branded can of water, CanO Water is the underdog fighting against the plastic giants.

In 2014, after seeing the devastating effects of plastic pollution in Thailand, three good friends, Josh, Ariel and Perry came together to imagine a better solution than plastic bottles of water. Obviously, tap water is the best alternative, but there had to be a more recyclable solution for on-the-go when you forget your beautifully designed reusable flask.

This set our founders on a journey to create the world's first branded can of water, a journey powered by purpose and fuelled by authenticity and passion.

Ditch the bottle – choose CanO Water

In 2019, only 7% of plastic was recycled, yes you read that right 7%! The more plastic we make, the more ends up in our forest, oceans and even our stomachs. Recycling plastic is clearly not working!

Why cans you may think?

It's the most recycled and recyclable packaging on the planet: it's recyclable forever and ever and ever and ever... The material never degrades, and it comes back in your hands in as little as 60 days.

In 2020, UK aluminium can recycling rates hit a record-breaking 82%, and contain on average 70% of recycled content.

Lastly, every drinks can recycled reduces the carbon footprint of the next. According to Metal Packaging Europe, the carbon footprint of a can (33cl) reduced by 30% in 10 years (2006-2016) – and it keeps reducing as recycling rates increase. Knowing that the lifespan of aluminium is forever, the carbon footprint over its forever lifetime will be minimum.

canowater.com

Four Pillars Gin

• • • •

FOUR PILLARS

Combining unmatched craft with style and personality, this distillery from Australia might just be the coolest gin brand on the planet right now.

Four Pillars Gin was founded in 2013 by three mates (Cam, Matt and Stu) with a shared love of great drinks and a shared belief that they could harness modern Australia's flavours and creativity to produce some of the world's best gin.

Based at their iconic Four Pillars Distillery in Melbourne's Yarra Valley, the brand combines a restless commitment to their craft (witness two consecutive IWSC 'International Gin Producer of the Year wins' and a trophy cabinet full of medals from around the world) with some of the most beautifully curated experiences, content and storytelling in the world of gin.

Their new drinks laboratory in Sydney's Surry Hills is just their latest demonstration of their passion for the intersection of gin, drinks, hospitality and design.

Gin makers above all

Restlessly creative, endlessly inventive and astonishingly delicious... Four Pillars Gin must be the most exciting gin brand in the world today.

Four Pillars have explored all the flavour possibilities of gin. From citrus and sweet to savoury and spicy, Four Pillars makes the perfect gin for every gin drink.

Their signature Rare Dry Gin uses fresh oranges in the distillation. And the Four Pillars team then make a gin-steamed marmalade with the leftover oranges. Their naturally sweet Bloody Shiraz Gin is made by soaking cool climate Yarra Valley Shiraz grapes in gin.

Their latest creation, the savoury Olive Leaf Gin, was inspired by the olive groves of Australia and uses freshly pressed extra virgin olive oil to make the perfect gin for a dirty martini or a Spanish-inspired Gintonic.

Four Pillars has placed drinks culture and deliciousness at the heart of their brand, even making a dedicated Spiced Negroni Gin. Ok, now we're very thirsty.

fourpillarsgin.com

Frieze

FRIEZE

Frieze is a media and events company that comprises three publications, frieze magazine, Frieze Masters Magazine and Frieze Week; and five international art fairs, Frieze London, Frieze LA, Frieze New York, Frieze Seoul (launching September 2022) and Frieze Masters; regular talks and summits, led by frieze editors; and frieze.com - the definitive resource for contemporary art and culture.

Frieze was founded in 1991 by Amanda Sharp, Matthew Slotover and Tom Gidley with the launch of frieze magazine, a leading magazine of contemporary art and culture. Sharp and Slotover established Frieze London in 2003, one of the world's most influential contemporary art fairs which takes place each October in The Regent's Park, London. In 2012, Frieze launched Frieze New York taking place in May; and Frieze Masters, which coincides with Frieze London in October and is dedicated to art from ancient to modern. In 2019, Frieze opened its first edition in Los Angeles, taking place in February.

A global community that champions art

Since 1991, Frieze has been creating moments for artists, galleries, institutions and art lovers to come together. You can now join this global community through Frieze Membership.

Frieze Membership supports a diverse and inclusive art community, with initiatives such as the Frieze x Deutsche Bank Emerging Curators Fellowship and the newly launched Frieze New Writers Programme, allowing aspiring writers to develop their skills with support from the Frieze editorial team and network of art professionals.

If you're looking to start or grow your personal art collection, Frieze 91 membership is designed to deepen your passion for art - offering a year-round programme of events and the insights you need.

Since May 2020 you can also access all Frieze art fairs from wherever you are in the world through Frieze Viewing Room – a pioneering digital initiative showcasing an extraordinary cross-section of artwork, from today's most exciting emerging artists to pioneering figures of the 20th century.

Left hand side page image: 'Frieze New York 2021 photos by Casey Kelbaugh'; Right hand page image: 'Frieze London 2019 photo by Nylind'

Hillier Bartley

hillier bartley

Hillier Bartley combines masculine elegance with rakish femininity and plays with the notion of mixing English aristocracy with street-style influences.

Founded in 2015 by Katie Hillier and Luella Bartley, the brand is a true reflection of everything the pair have learnt as designers. It is defiant and purist, sophisticated while retaining the punkish attitude of youth, irreverent by nature while maturing into refinement. A play between juxtapositions; resulting in androgynous, luxurious, and iconic design with a gender-inclusive approach.

An uncompromising commitment to craftsmanship, considered design, luxurious materials, and precise attention to detail runs through each collection. Hillier Bartley is a brand that embodies luxury with attitude.

Operating where possible with zero waste throughout the development and manufacturing process, ensuring that the greatest care is taken throughout every stage and process in order to produce accessories to the highest standard.

Photography: David Sims

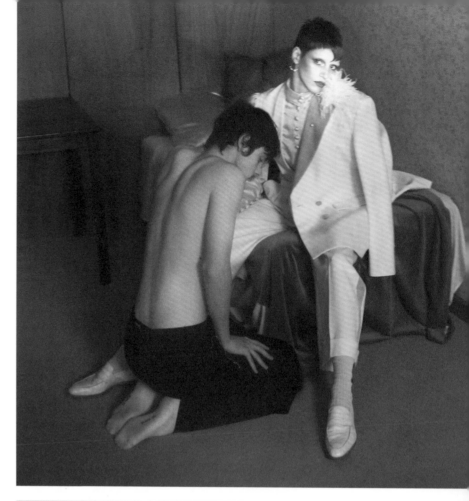

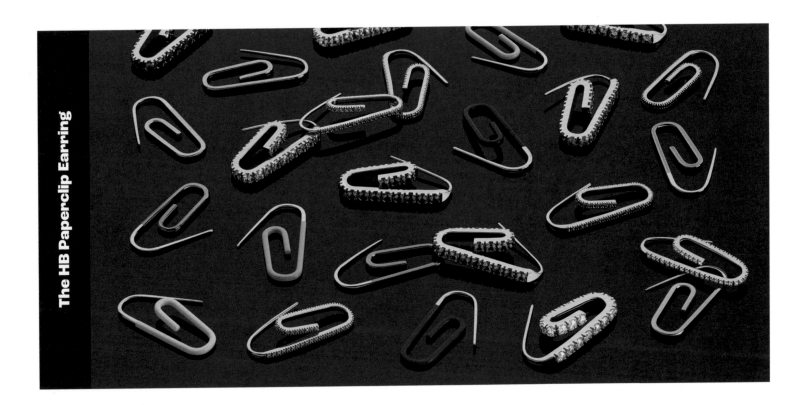

The icon

Introduced by Katie and Luella, Hillier Bartley has long celebrated the paperclip; re-interpreting this D.I.Y. symbol as refined, elevated jewellery, irreverence mixes with everyday luxury.

The HB Paperclip Earring has long been the figurehead of Hillier Bartley's exploration into subverting mundane objects. An icon of the brand, the paperclip is a simple, everyday token given a sublime elevation to become a precious and prized piece of jewellery that can be worn in a multitude of ways, from the elegant and ladylike to the glam and louche.

From it's introduction in 2016, it has become shorthand for the duos subversive and witty approach to designing with an English irreverence that evokes counter cultures and street influences, and has been re-imagined in a multitude of materials and finishes.

Photography: Toby McFarlan Pond

Home Grown Club

London's Leading Business Club

Home Grown is a private members' club that provides entrepreneurial pioneers with unique resources to unlock the true value of their business potential. It is a global community of experienced entrepreneurs, sophisticated investors and trusted advisors.

Set in a stunning six story Georgian building in the heart of Marylebone, Home Grown offers a space for like-minded people to network, entertain and grow. With 35 luxurious bedrooms offering unrivalled access to the city, innovative business lounges, bars, pitching suites and a stylish restaurant, Home Grown hosts a variety of spaces to support growth entrepreneurs and investors on their journey to success.

Home Grown boasts spaces to encourage discussion, both formal and informal. Here you can speak with fellow entrepreneurs in the study café or hire one of our private meeting rooms. Dine in our quintessentially British restaurant from breakfast right through till dinner.

With a focus on seasonal, ingredients sourced from independent, and, where possible, local suppliers, the menus are wholesome, with a touch of experimental.

For Business as Unusual

Home Grown, as part of the Home House Collection, offers a space for exclusive and unrivalled access to the brightest minds in London's thriving business community.

As many entrepreneurs will know, it can get lonely at the top and having an established network comes with a number of benefits, including having people that can help you through pivotal moments and processes.

Home Grown is here to support its members' needs from scaling a business, through to providing a network of investors and industry experts.

Home Grown's events series has been curated to inspire lively debate and disrupt thinking with qualified opinion based on experience. They aim to help businesses grow by understanding their key needs and providing dynamic content to mirror this. The Home Grown programme of events includes unrivalled insight and access to: Talent and Skills, Markets, Finance, Leadership, Infrastructure, Community and Wellbeing.

Institute of Contemporary Arts

ICA

Radical arts since 1946.

Supporting pressing debates in contemporary culture through film, visual arts, music, performance and spoken word.

The ICA presents a far-reaching programme at our iconic central London building and online: new visual art in our extensive exhibition spaces, a full film calendar across two cinemas, performances and symposia in the ICA Theatre and much more besides. We encourage different modes of cultural production to thrive on mutual engagement with one another while interrogating what it means to live in our world today, addressing issues as diverse as globalisation, race, gender, sexuality, political populism and environmental catastrophe.

ica.art

Jaguar

Since the first Jaguar was produced in 1935, we have pushed the boundaries of what is possible, inspired by our founder, Sir William Lyons.

He insisted that every Jaguar produced combined performance and beauty like no other. His uncompromising vision set new benchmarks that we still live by.

Today's world-class Jaguar model range comprises two stylish saloons, three performance SUVs - including our all-electric I-PACE, and our iconic F-TYPE sports car. The Jaguar DNA is instantly recognisable across our range – there is an unmistakable purity of line that runs through all our models. Agile and powerful; sleek and seductive; confident and instinctive: all these qualities are reflected in our cars.

From 2025, Jaguar will become a pure electric modern luxury brand with a dramatically beautiful new portfolio of emotionally engaging designs and pioneering next-generation technologies. The journey towards electrification is underway with a range of mild and plug-in hybrid and full-electric models available today.

The future of modern luxury, reimagined

Set against a canvas of true sustainability, Jaguar has become a more agile creator of the world's most desirable luxury vehicles and services for the most discerning of customers.

Sustainability that delivers a new benchmark in environmental and societal impact for the luxury sector is at the heart of Jaguar and is shaping our exciting future.

By the middle of the decade, Jaguar will have undergone a renaissance to emerge as a pure electric luxury brand with a dramatically beautiful new portfolio of emotionally engaging designs and pioneering next-generation technologies.

By 2030, it's anticipated that 100% of Jaguar vehicles will be electric and that Jaguar Land Rover will achieve net-zero carbon emissions across its supply chain, products, and operations by 2039.

Today, we exist to make life extraordinary and strive to leave our customers feeling unique and rewarded by creating dramatically beautiful automotive experiences, and that will continue to be our philosophy as we reimagine our future.

Ketel One Botanical

Natural Botanicals. Fresh taste.

Made with Ketel One Vodka, distilled with natural botanicals and fruit essences.

Ketel One Botanical, available in 3 varietals, has a beautifully crisp and refreshing taste.

When mixed with soda water, you can enjoy the perfect Ketel One Botanical spritz with 40% less calories than a glass of white wine*. Perfect for any Aperitivo moment. There's nothing quite like the long, lazy lunches & brunches, BBQ's or picnics in the park with the people we love. Or that refreshing after-work drink. Laughter, swapping stories and opinions about the things we care about.

*82 calories based on a 50ml measured serving and 150ml of soda water.

ketelone.com/botanical

Kiss the Moon

Let's talk beauty sleep

Night-time aromatherapy to help you to sleep beautifully & wake up feeling gorgeous.

Born in 2014 by founder Jo Foster to help get her own sleep back on track, Kiss the Moon has taken nature's most relaxing essential oils and created four unique aromatherapy blends specially designed to help you get more out of your night's sleep.

The award-winning product range includes night-time skincare, bath & body products and home fragrance designed to help you create your perfect nightly wind-down routine. Based in the North Yorkshire countryside, Kiss the Moon recently opened their first Sleep Boutique near their home town of Richmond. Everything created there is 100% natural, cruelty free and suitable for vegans.

London Fields Brewery

One of the early new wave breweries to emerge in London a decade ago, London Fields has re-established itself at the vanguard of the capital's modern beer scene.

As the story goes, in the brewery's early days during the London Riots of 2011, the owners barricaded themselves into the railway arch to protect their precious new brew kit.

They created a beer called Love Not War, a positive response to the strife that hit East London's Hackney borough particularly hard.

This ethos of creativity through adversity has stood the brewery in good stead over the past decade, from its previous status as the hip Hackney hangout of Hollywood celebs, to ensuing scandals, the 'big brewer' takeover by Carlsberg and Brooklyn Brewery, then lockdown where the brewery flipped its entire model within days to become a beer delivery specialist both nationwide and hyper-locally. London Fields has also supported its cultural partners, notably the iconic Roundhouse in Camden, via a fundraising collaboration beer.

Core range created by Luke McLean

Love Not War

London Fields makes modern beer that is accessible and 'smashable' according to Head Brewer Talfryn Provis-Evans. The brewery can make any beer style, from classic lagers to mixed fermentation sours and hazy IPAs.

"We're part of the community. It keeps us honest and we listen to our audience with real attention to detail. The brewers consistently make great beer, our taproom doubles as an off-licence and e-commerce hub, and we keep the brand fun through difficult times" says Dipak Nayar, CCO of London Fields.

Luke Mclean creates the brand's distinctive psychedelic pop art, seen on can designs, merch and more. The core range artwork, including the bestselling Hackney Hopster pale ale, are inspired by Luke's last twenty odd years of living in East London.

For Luke, Shoreditch Triangle's voodoo queen represents the party vibes of the early 2000s. "Pretty much anything goes, and once inside the 'Triangle' – you went missing – no-one would hear from you for days", says the artist.

With those frolics overdue a return, you should grab a pint of London Fields and embrace the excitement of East London.

onefinestay

The finest stays

Pairing our guests with the world's most desirable private homes, villas and chalets, with one of a kind service to create tailored experiences.

Founded in 2010 and now part of Accor, its 5000, curated and inspected homes are hand-picked for their prime locations, space, character and comfort. From beachside estates to historic terraced homes, countryside villas and mountain chalets, onefinestay helps guests find their ideal home-from-home, whilst every stay is professionally managed to ensure an effortless and enjoyable rental experience. This includes a personal welcome, 24/7 guest support, extensive housekeeping and dedicated concierge services. Its unique approach to short and medium-term renting appeals to anyone looking for a private place to stay and a premium hospitality experience to match.

Rock Rose Gin

ROCK ROSE
PREMIUM SCOTTISH GIN

Scottish Gin

Dunnet Bay Distillery is the stylish, sustainable spirits company which created multi-award-winning Rock Rose Gin.

From the most northerly coast of mainland Scotland, the eco-friendly, family-owned business runs its own distillery, hand-crafting a range of Rock Rose Gins and Holy Grass Vodka, reflecting the purity and beauty of the Scottish coastline.

These elegant and subtle spirits celebrate the heritage and provenance of Caithness using many locally foraged and home-grown botanicals to create exceptional, eco-friendly spirits.

This is the first company in its sector to offer spirits in recyclable pouches to refill their iconic ceramic bottles.

Sea Containers London

SEA CONTAINERS
LONDON

Lifestyle hotel on the Southbank

A destination where glamour meets brutalism – your London anchor on the River Thames.

Based on London's famed Southbank, Sea Containers London designed under the creative direction of Tom Dixon, offers 359 bedrooms, with river-facing suites, a ground-floor award-winning cocktail bar named Lyaness, a rooftop bar called 12th Knot overlooking the River Thames and St Paul's, and to top it all of an award-winning subterranean spa called agua London with its own sustainable and seasonal product and treatment range.

With the Tate Modern, National Theatre, Borough Market and the Southbank Centre all within walking distance to the hotel, it makes a great spot for some R&R and exploration of some of London's greatest treasures.

Secret Cinema

SECRETCINEMA

"Walking into a Secret Cinema event is akin to walking into a festival that exists only to celebrate a single movie." — Wired

Imagine being able to step into your favourite film. To not only walk through the world but play a part in how the story unfolds. Welcome to the spectacular world of Secret Cinema.

With a little bit of magic and a whole lot of imagination, the pioneers of immersive entertainment bring your favourite stories to life through experiences of epic proportions.

When arriving at a secret location you're struck by the bewildering sight of hundreds of people dressed as part of the film. Equipped with bespoke backstories and missions, you don't know who's the actor and who's the audience.

For the next hours, you can get completely swept up in another reality as you roam iconic life-sized locations, uncover hidden rooms, explore new plots, and enjoy familiar bars and restaurants. Each person has a unique journey and leaves with indelible memories. Whether you want to be at the heart of the action, or simply mesmerised by the spectacle, your story awaits.

"I have traded with jawas; performed in 1899 Montmartre; danced in acid rain; become a double agent... Would I recommend Secret Cinema? I'd bloody move in if they let me!"

Created by Fabien Riggall in 2007, Secret Cinema has revolutionised the way audiences experience culture and live entertainment. Known as the must-attend events for all social calendars, Secret Cinema hasn't gained a cult following for nothing. They do what so many are afraid to do; let the audience decide how the story unfolds.

With innovation at the core and 50+ productions in their arsenal, Secret Cinema never fails to surprise. We've seen them bring to life everything from iconic films like Blade Runner and Star Wars to smash-hit tv-series like Stranger Things and Bridgerton to music albums like Laura Marling.

Constantly pushing the boundaries of what's possible, they now have their eyes set on the world of gaming...

Whether it is spine-chilling missions or dazzling parties, tear-jerking tragedies or euphoric adventures, we cannot wait for what's next.

secretcinema.org

Tatty Devine

Tatty Devine is the go-to brand for original, fun, acrylic statement jewellery, and was founded in the heart of East London in 1999 by Harriet Vine MBE and Rosie Wolfenden MBE after graduating from Chelsea School of Art. All jewellery is still designed and handmade in house by a female-led team.

They often collaborate with artists, designers, and their favourite cultural spaces to create special collections throughout the year. All of Tatty Devine's collections are sold online and in their London store in Covent Garden. New designs and iconic pieces from their archive are highly coveted and collected by a loyal fan base from all over the world and discovered by new customers every day.

"We've come to the conclusion that our purpose is to bring joy"
— Rosie Wolfenden MBE

Tatty Devine jewellery carries a strong feminist message and is known for making a statement and starting conversations.

Since 2018, Tatty Devine have partnered with the Fawcett Society, the UK's leading charity campaigning for advancement in gender equality and women's rights.

Fawcett Society have received £3 for every piece sold amounting to nearly £15,000 in 2.5 years. In response to the 2020 pandemic, Tatty Devine donated to Young Women's Trust emergency fund and in January 2021 launched a collection featuring original illustrations by Venus Libido to continue their donations to help achieve economic justice for young women.

Collaborators with some of the biggest cultural institutions in the UK, as well as celebrated artists and musicians alike. This year, Tatty Devine launched an exclusive range of jewellery for the V&A's 'Curiouser and Curiouser' exhibition, has collaborated with renowned artist and designer Morag Myerscough and is working with independent music label Heavenly Recordings on original merchandise for emerging female artists.

tattydevine.com

The Groucho Club

Original private members club for the arts and media

A world-renowned arts & media private members club, based in Soho, London. Created in the 1980s by a group of mostly women publishers as an antidote to the stuffy gentlemen's clubs. The Groucho Club remains a bastion and refuge for arts, literature and media folk in the bohemian heart of London's West End due to our celebrated restaurants and bars, famous event and part room hire, (infamous) bedrooms, exclusive member services and feeling of cosy intimacy.

Images credits from left to right: Rob and Nick Carter, "Read Colours Not Words, From Blue to Orange", 2009, unique multi-coloured neon (47 x 118 x 8 in | 119 x 300 x 20 cm); Richard Lewisohn for The Groucho Club; Main Bar Piano, Artwork by Sir Peter Blake; Left page: Richard Lewisohn for The Groucho Club.

thegrouchoclub.com

The Hepworth Wakefield

THE HEPWORTH WAKEFIELD

The Hepworth Wakefield is an art gallery designed by the acclaimed David Chipperfield Architects and located in the heart of Yorkshire.

Alongside the gallery is a beautiful public garden, free for all to enjoy, designed by the renowned landscape architect, Tom Stuart-Smith.

Named after Barbara Hepworth, one of the most important artists of the 20th century who was born and brought up in Wakefield, The Hepworth Wakefield creates unforgettable art experiences for all. It was awarded Art Fund Museum of the Year 2017 and is one of the most visited art galleries outside of London.

It presents major temporary exhibitions of the best international modern and contemporary art and runs a dynamic outreach and engagement programme with local communities and schools. It is home to Wakefield's growing art collection – an impressive compendium of modern British and contemporary art. There are also dedicated galleries exploring Hepworth's art and working process and outdoor sculptures in the garden.

The Hepworth Wakefield is 'one of the UK's most important – and youngest – contemporary art centres' — Kinfolk

The Hepworth Wakefield is a registered charity that works with a range of funders and corporate partners in order to present its diverse exhibition programme and deliver its learning and outreach work.

Collaborations with some of the UK's best artists, designers and makers to create exclusive products for its shop, including artist editions, make the Hepworth Wakefield Shop the go-to place for any discerning buyer.

A vibrant and well-established programme of fairs and markets including Print Fair, Ceramics Fair and Christmas Market are hosted on-site and online. These events support makers around the country, enabling them to sell direct to The Hepworth's large audiences.

With over 1,600 square metres of light-filled gallery spaces, versatile event spaces and inspiring art, the dramatic building and stunning garden are available to hire for filming, photo shoots, product launches, special events and weddings.

hepworthwakefield.org

Tony's Chocolonely

Together we'll make 100% slave free the norm in chocolate.

There are currently 1.56 million children working illegally and at least 30,000 instances of modern slavery on farms in Ghana and Ivory Coast where 60% of the world's cocoa comes from. Pretty shocking right?

The root cause of this problem is poverty. Cocoa farmers and their families live way below the poverty line and can't afford to pay for labour because the biggest chocolate companies don't pay enough for their cocoa.

At Tony's we don't think the human beings at the start of the cocoa supply chain should be exploited to make a sweet luxury, so we're doing things differently. We deliberately source from Ghana and Ivory Coast where the problem is worst so that we can change it from the inside.

We've developed 5 sourcing principles and believe that when all 5 are in place (no cherry-picking) you can eradicate illegal labour from your supply chain. We've made this model open source through Tony's Open Chain and invite all chocolate companies to join us in changing the industry for the better.

Our bars are unequally divided, like the chocolate industry

An impact company that makes chocolate

With incredibly tasty chocolate, we lead by example to show the world that chocolate can be made differently: in taste, packaging and the way you do business with cocoa farmers.

Tony's was started in 2005 by a team of Dutch journalists who were outraged to learn about the hidden human rights violations in the chocolate industry. When the biggest chocolate companies wouldn't work with them to fix it they took matters into their own hands and created the first Tony's Chocolonely bar – our milk chocolate in an alarming red wrapper. Since then we have grown to be the number 1 chocolate brand in The Netherlands, the fastest-growing chocolate brand in the UK and are now stocked in over 30+ countries worldwide.

But success for us isn't selling chocolate bars – they are just a means to our goal. And we can't achieve that mission alone. The more people who join us and share our story, the sooner 100% slave-free will become the norm in chocolate.

The choice is yours, are you in?

tonyschocolonely.com

Vita Coco

17 years ago during a casual outing to a NYC bar, childhood friends Ira Liran and Mike Kirban met two young women from Brazil.

When asked what they missed most about their country, the ladies said 'agua de coco', which they described as the most delicious and nutritious drink in the world. Two months later they hopped on a plane to Brazil with a plan to bring coconut water to the US...Vita Coco was born.

The brand quickly grew into a celebrity favourite with big-name investors including Madonna, Matthew McConaughey and Rihanna (to name a few).

In recent years, Vita Coco has launched several super exciting innovations including Impossible To Hate Pressed coconut water, CBD infused sparkling coconut water and most recently Vita Coco Haircare with 3 ranges including Scalp, Nourish and Repair – each offering a shampoo, conditioner and a treatment.

Vita Coco has become known for challenging big brands through disruptive marketing whilst remaining committed to sustainability.

More than just coconuts!

Vita Coco has grown into more than just a business and in 2019 became B-Corp certified, with a commitment to the B-Corp values of balancing profit with purpose.

Vita Coco strives to operate in a sustainable way across the entire supply chain. Starting with the farmers, the Vita Coco Project works alongside them to empower and enable them to develop sustainable farming techniques. It has an overall goal of raising 1 million farmers out of poverty.

Alongside positively impacting the farmers who grow the coconuts, Vita Coco also works to support their employees along the whole supply chain, right up to head office through various wellness schemes and employee benefits.

Vita Coco strives to be a market leader in inclusivity and diversity and supports charities with similar goals to push this agenda further.

Wildsmith Skin

WILDSMITH

S K I N

England, MMXVIII.

RADICAL BOTANY

Clinically proven, natural skincare.

At Wildsmith Skin, we make clinically proven, natural and effective skincare. We blend the very best of science and nature using powerful bio-actives and nutrient-rich botanicals to deliver targeted performance and great results. We are passionate about skin health and pack our products with antioxidants and anti-inflammatories - we call our approach Radical Botany.

Our guiding light at Wildsmith Skin is the progressive horticulturalist, William Walker Wildsmith. During the late nineteenth century, Wildsmith created the gardens and arboretum of Heckfield Place. The idyllic, English estate, with its biodynamic market garden, is our spiritual home and source of constant inspiration. Wildsmith's radical approach to horticulture, in particular the trees he lovingly planted, continue to shape our philosophy to skincare. True to our ethos 'Made by Many' we work with sustainable growers to provide the most nutrient-rich botanicals and essential oils that our experts incorporate into the very latest in progressive and effective natural skincare technology.

Radical Botany

Our products go through rigorous, Independent Clinical and Consumer user Trials. We ensure that we bring the finest and most beneficial natural ingredients to each product.

We are committed to sustainable and environmentally sensitive practices. Striving to ensure a circular economy, we were one of the first luxury beauty brands to use Mycelium packaging, feeding the very soil from which we grow our own ingredients. We are committed to using recyclable glass, paper and aluminium.

Our award-winning Nourishing Cleansing Balm (above) is the cornerstone of our range. We think of it as 'A Spa in a Jar' for its ability to take both your skin and senses to another level.

Skin health and formula integrity are at the heart of everything we do. We take great pride in our formulas, pushing the boundaries of what skin care can deliver, using organic and growing our own ingredients, where possible.

Exploring our range is an inspiring sensory experience where ingredients connect us back to nature and technology creates effective results.

About the CoolBrands® selection process

CoolBrands® is an initiative to identify and pay tribute to the nation's coolest brands, running since 2001.

After a few years gap, CoolBrands® returned, and as ever brands do not apply or pay to be considered.

The selection process is independently administered by The Centre for Brand Analysis (TCBA), who also manage the Superbrands research programme, centred more on mainstream brands.

From the thousands of brands initially identified for consideration, a comprehensive final shortlist of 1,540 brands across 72 sector and sub-sectors was compiled using a wide range of quantitative and qualitative sources.

The list is eclectic and includes both established and challenger brands with differing consumer profiles and fame. How big a brand is, or how long it has been operating, was not in itself important to being considered for the final list.

The extensive shortlist of brands was voted on by an independent and voluntary council of 49 experts and influencers convened by TCBA. Leaders from across multiple fields from technology to fashion, and from beauty to health & wellbeing provided breadth of expertise and knowledge.

Council members individually awarded each brand a rating from 1-10 and were not allowed to score brands with which they have an association or are in competition with.

Brands were sorted into categories, to help individuals evaluate brands against their peers. As this is a UK orientated project, individuals were asked to consider the brands credentials in the UK only, so whether a brand is large or well-regarded internationally was not something individuals had to consider.

Cool is subjective and personal, so naturally individuals only scored brands with which they were very familiar.

As perception of what defines cool and what brands are cool vary greater from one person to the next, the expert council were not given a tight definition of what constitutes cool.

We were interested in each person's feelings about each brand now relative to their own criteria of what makes a brand cool. Nevertheless, the following five influential factors were outlined to the voters, who were asked to bear these in mind when scoring:

1 Original

Does the brand stand-out from rivals, is it distinctive in its product, styling or marketing, and does the voter believe it treads its own path rather than following others

2 Innovative

Is the brand constantly refreshing and developing, proving adaptable and flexible, perhaps driving market changes based on shifting customer demands

3 Authentic

Does the brand have a clear and evident underlying purpose and values, and does it feel genuinely passionate about what it does

4 Desirable

Is there a lustre for the brand compared to peers, do people seek it out and is there excitement about new product and services they release

5 Responsible

Is the brand more than a nice product or service well presented. Is it fundamentally a good corporate citizen, for example treating employees well, focusing on genuine sustainability, while embracing positive human values and equality

Stephen Cheliotis

CEO, The Centre for Brand Analysis (TCBA)

Chair Superbrands and CoolBrands® Councils

Since starting his career at Brand Finance, Stephen has provided robust research, trends & insights, and strategic branding advice to both established and challenger brands across a wide variety of B2B and B2C sectors.

Stephen also develops research studies, white papers, and proprietary models for marketing agencies.

A regular commentator on CNN, the BBC and Sky among others, Stephen encourages the next generation of marketers as a visiting professor and also a judge for the Marketing Academy scholarship.

About TCBA

TCBA undertakes a wide range of research, brand evaluation and brand strategy projects across both business-to-consumer and business-to-business sectors.

Projects range from brand trackers and internal brand equity diagnostics to complete 360-stakeholder studies developing a new brand positioning.

The Centre's audit and consultancy services are orientated around supplying practical and robust research, evidence and insights that shape brand and business strategy, aid creativity and effectiveness, and ultimately enhance brand reputation and underlying business growth.

TCBA works directly with brand owners, working in sectors as diverse as higher education to fashion retail, and from steel manufacturing to government services. TCBA works for both established global brands and smaller challenger brands.

TCBA also work through marketing services providers, including design, PR, digital and content agencies. TCBA has developed research studies, white papers and proprietary tools for marketing agencies. Studies include the Emotion100, exploring how brands build emotional engagement, Talkonomic, exploring the underlying drivers of advocacy, and Headspace, which measures brand's mental market share across categories.

Based on the collective scores of the 49 council members, the top 20 CoolBrands® for this year were:

Rank	Brand name	Category	Council index
1	Tony's Chocolonely	Food – Chocolate	100.0
2	Barbican	Experiences – Museums & Galleries	97.4
3	Glastonbury	Experiences – Festivals & Events	96.8
4	Haeckels	Beauty – Skincare	96.7
5	The Hepworth Wakefield	Experiences – Museums & Galleries	96.0
6	Brat	Food – Restaurants Stand Alone	96.0
7	Apple	Technology – General	95.8
8	Monmouth Coffee Company	Drinks – Coffee & Tea	95.0
9	Ottolenghi	Food – Bakeries, Coffee Shops & Food to Go	94.3
10	Tate	Experiences – Museums & Galleries	94.1

Of this year's top 20 only Apple (1st), Glastonbury (2nd) and Spotify (7th) featured in the top 20 in the last iteration of the research, conducted back in 2016-17, although direct comparisons are difficult due to time, and changes in the methodology and composition of the council, list etc.

Rank	Brand name	Category	Council index
11	Frieze	Experiences – Festivals & Events	94.0
12	Leica	Technology – Vision	93.6
13	The V&A	Experiences – Museums & Galleries	93.5
14	Vitra	Home – Hard Furnishing	93.5
15	TED	Tuition & Learning	93.4
16	Pooky	Home – Decorating, Lighting & Soft Furnishings	93.2
17	method	Home – Household Goods	93.2
18	Spotify	Media – Content & Streaming Services	93.2
19	YSP (Yorkshire Sculpture Park)	Experiences – Museums & Galleries	93.0
20	Hauser & Wirth	Experiences – Museums & Galleries	92.9

Expert council

James Balfour

Co-founder, 1Rebel

James Balfour, Co-Founder of 1Rebel. James left investment banking in 2007 to complete his lifelong dream of climbing Mount Everest making him one of the youngest Briton's to do so.

Since then, James has completed many expeditions including leading a team to the South Pole. In 2007 James joined forces with his father to co-found Jatomi fitness. After 4 years in Eastern Europe, James moved to Malaysia to grow the business as CEO of Asia.

In 2015, alongside his business partner Giles Dean, James went on to found 1Rebel which now has clubs in the UK, Middle East and Australia.

Tim Beaumont

Founder, Beaumont London

Tim originally founded Beaumont Communications in 2011 and as the company approached its tenth anniversary this year, it rebranded to 'epilogue' marking a period of expansion and promotions. epilogue specialises in developing new talent and maintaining and protecting established names. The company has four divisions - 'Drama', 'Broadcast', 'Experts' and 'Podcasts', a part of the business that handles series publicity for podcasts. Clients include Emily Beecham, Greg Wise, Rakie Ayola, Joe Dempsie, Indira Varma, Laura Donnelly and Martin Compston, chef and restaurateur Gizzi Erskine, charity CEO and model Noëlla Coursaris Musunka, Jamie Laing and his podcast 'Private Parts', Simon Rimmer and his podcast 'Grilling'.

John Booth

Artist

London-based illustrator, ceramicist and textile designer, John Booth is renowned for his graphic aesthetic featuring multi-layered collages of textures and colours.

His instinctive, un-laboured collage techniques combined with painted and drawn elements bring together rough-and-ready textures with luminous colours for a touching sensitivity.

More recently, Booth has been focusing on making interior and art-based objects with Ian McIntyre under their collaborative platform Supergroup.

Booth's diverse works feature in the fashion world, magazine covers, restaurant walls and in museum collections.

Edith Bowman

DJ, radio presenter & television personality

Edith Bowman has worked as a TV and Radio broadcaster for over 20 years. Her radio work has spanned all the major stations, presenting shows on BBC Radio 1, 2, 6 and 5Live as well as Virgin Radio.

As a TV host and producer she has fronted a versatile mix of shows for BBC, Channel 4, Sky Arts, MTV. From hosting music festival coverage to the BAFTA Awards 2021, Edith has incorporated her genuine passion for music and film in to her work. In 2016 she launched her own podcast "Soundtracking" allowing her to combine both loves – the go to podcast for film and music lovers.

Charlie Casley-Hayford

Menswear designer and co-founder

Casely-Hayford is a leading London-based fashion brand founded by father and son duo the late Joe Casely-Hayford OBE and Charlie Casely-Hayford in 2009. The Bespoke House skilfully merges modern tailoring nuances with British subcultural references to craft a purposeful modular wardrobe centred around slow fashion.

Each collection is designed and cut from studios in both London and Tokyo. Fine English and Japanese fabrics are combined with the signature House cut and construction to create a unique design statement. Integral to the brand's DNA is its link to the UK and international music scene.

Dominic Cools-Lartigue

Founder, Street Feast

Dominic Cools-Lartigue is the founder of Street Feast, London's pioneering street food market. When he sold Street Feast in 2015, more than 20,000 people a week were attending his venues.

Prior to this Dominic spent fifteen years in the music industry putting on events all over the world from Ibiza to Miami. In March 2020 when London went into its first lockdown Dominic set up A Plate For London who have fed over 35,000 people in need. In autumn 2020 Dominic launched the Tramshed Project, in Shoreditch which The Telegraph referred to as "the future of dining out".

Josh Cuthbert

Model & creative

Model, presenter and singer Josh Cuthbert rose to prominence in 2012 with chart topping boy band Union J, and has since gone on to have a successful career in fashion, broadcasting and as an online creative. He has built a strong social presence which led to him regularly collaborating with high-end luxury brands including; Kooples, Hugo Boss, Jimmy Choo and this year became an ambassador for Givenchy.

In addition to this, Josh had his own show on Heat Radio for two years from 2017, was a contestant and finalist on BBC's Celebrity Master Chef, and in 2018 was on the cover of Men's Fitness where he shared his own physical and mental wellbeing journey.

DJ Spoony

DJ, Radio presenter & television personality

DJ Spoony is a British garage DJ and radio presenter. Spoony's career started on pirate radio station London Underground, forming the trio the Dreem Teem with Mikee B and Timmi Magic. With the Dreem Teem, he joined Kiss 100 in 1997, followed by bringing UK garage nationally to BBC Radio 1 in January 2000. Spoony was a resident DJ at the UK's top garage and R&B club night 'Twice as Nice' for 7 years, mixing and compiling three gold selling compilation albums for the brand. He has had residencies in Ibiza and Ayia Napa for over 20 years. You can currently catch him 'live streaming' on Twitch, hosting a football show across the world's TV for the Premier League on occasionally on Radio 2

Erin Doherty

Actor

Nicola Fontanella

Founder, Argent Design

Michael Fox

Actor

Glyn Fussell

Co-creator of Sink the Pink & Presenter

Erin was a 2018 Screen International Star of Tomorrow and a 2018 Evening Standard Rising Star. In 2020, Erin was honoured at the Newport Beach Film Festival as 'Breakout Honouree' following her role of Princess Anne. Doherty is a highly respected theatre actress, playing leads in some of the best houses across the UK.

In 2017, Erin appeared in BAFTA Award-winning writer Jack Thorne's Junkyard. Later that year she took on the leading role in Aykbourn's The Divide at the Edinburgh International Festival to critical acclaim, and The Young Vic's one woman show My Name is Rachel Corrie again won her plaudits.

Nicola completed her studies in London and worked with Harrods Design Studio to develop her interior design skills; she then explored the hospitality design sector and dealt with international commercial projects, hotels and restaurants. She spent two years on site in Turkey, overseeing and designing the interior of the Intercontinental Hotel and worked with many international HNWI's on various residential schemes in locations worldwide.

Nicola founded Argent Design in 1997 and since her first year of trading quickly gained a solid client-base of private individuals of both UK and international reputable standing.

Michael trained at the Central School of Speech and Drama on the Collaborative and Devised Theatre course.

He starred as Andy Parker in ITV's Downton Abbey, and will soon begin shooting the second Downton Abbey Movie. Michael has had roles in television drama's including Midsomer Murders, Endeavour, The Ark opposite David Threlfall and Marvellous alongside Toby Jones. Michael has appeared on the big screen in Christopher Nolan's Academy Award winning film Dunkirk. Michael has also performed onstage in A Lie Of The Mind and in the Chichester Festival Theatre's production of Ibsen's An Enemy Of The People.

Glyn is most well-known for being a co-founder of Sink the Pink – one of the largest LGBTQ+ events in the UK which has been running for almost twelve years, and is also a brand in its own right. Glyn is also co-founder of creative agency East Creative, home to Mighty Hoopla Festival & Noisy Kitchen DJ agency.

As well as this, Glyn has hosted the hugely popular BBC Sounds podcast Radio 1's Drag Queens Den.

David Gandy
Model

Described as the world's most successful male supermodel, David has just celebrated his 20 years in the fashion industry. Adorning hundreds of magazine covers, billboards, as well as the face of numerous now iconic campaigns. He continues to build his substantial portfolio of brands with investments in many British start-ups, as well as continuing his Ambassador and members role for the British Fashion Council and London Fashion Week Men's.

David maintains his Ambassador roles for many charities including Style for Soldiers, Battersea Dogs & Cats Home, Wild at Heart and Achievement For All.

Maria Hatzistefanis
Founder, RODIAL

Maria Hatzistefanis is founder of Rodial, entrepreneur, best-selling author and podcaster. Maria made her author debut in 2017 with her best-selling book – How To Be An Overnight Success, released her second book How To Make It Happen last year, and has a third book landing in 2021.

Maria boasts 800K+ follows on social media using the platforms to inspire and motivate her audience. Her podcast, Overnight Success is a regular in the iTunes charts. Maria is a Patron to the British Fashion Council and sits on the panel for the BFC Vogue Fashion Fund.

Katie Hillier
Creative director & accessories designer

For nearly twenty years, Katie Hillier has worked creatively to produce bags, jewellery, accessories and RTW, that fuse classic British irreverent style with high-end luxury.

Hillier has worked on many creative collaborations, including of course, Luella Bartley with whom she runs the cool luxury label, Hillier Bartley.

Her passionate and visceral reaction to ideas means simple gestures become elevated, eventually turning into iconic shapes and products; the paperclip earring, her infamous Bunny Bag.

Henry Holland
Designer

Henry Holland is an English fashion designer, businessman and blogger from Greater Manchester.

Henry is a graduate of the BA Journalism course at the London College of Communication and has worked for the following publications: the teenage Sneak magazine (fashion section), Smash Hits and Bliss.

Prior to the launch of his own company, Holland gained attention with his Fashion Groupies T-shirt designs.

Tom Honeyands

The Tech Chap

Tom Honeyands is the tech guru who has gained fame for his 'The Tech Chap' YouTube channel. He has earned more than 179 million views for his reviews, unboxings and tutorials for PC, phones, laptops and high-end car tech.

Seema Jaswal

Sports presenter & event host

Seema Jaswal is one of the industry's most sought-after Sports Presenters, currently presenting BT Sports coverage of the UEFA Champions League, Premier League's Match-Day Live coverage, ITV'S International football and BBC Snooker's Triple Crown events. Seema has presented various tournaments, including the UEFA Champions League 2020, Cricket World Cup 2019 and FIFA World Cup 2018. She has also hosted events including the Rugby League World Cup Draw 2021 at Buckingham Palace with Prince Harry. She has been awarded Sport's Journalist of the year at the Asian Media Awards 2018 and the Media Award at the Asian Football Awards 2017.

David Jonsson

Actor

David Jonsson is a British actor who has starred in roles across film, TV and theatre. Following a scholarship from Warner Bros. to attend RADA, David's first role out of drama school was Davison in MARY STUART at the Almeida. He recently starred in Yomi Sode's ...AND BREATHE at the Almeida. David was most recently seen in the HBO/BBC series INDUSTRY and will reprise his role of Gus for the second series. He was named on Digital Spy's Digital Spy Rising: 30 Black British stars of tomorrow.

Chanté Joseph

Writer & broadcaster

Chanté is a freelance writer, digital content producer and host of Channel 4's How Not To Be Racist & The Face Magazine's 'My Public Me' Podcast. Chanté frequently writes for platforms including British Vogue, Complex, The Guardian, The I Paper, Huffington Post, VICE, Gal-dem, Soho House and more.

She has recently hosted live streams for Tik Tok and collaborated with brands such as Bumble, adidas, Spotify and Youtube. Chanté is also currently writing for her first book A Quick Ting On: The Black British Power Movement, due out in 2021.

Leyla Kazim
Broadcaster & presenter

Roman Kemp
Radio host & broadcaster

Millie Kendall
CEO, British Beauty Council

Ferdinand Kingsley
Actor

Leyla is a presenter, broadcaster, speaker, reporter and digital creator, as well as the founder of the authoritative online brand The Cutlery Chronicles, specialising in travel and food.

She travels to eat and spent 2015 on one big trip tasting her way around the world. Leyla drew on this catalogue of culinary experiences to co-create Lonely Planet's book: The Ultimate Eatlist, The World's Top 500 Food Experiences (2018).

Part of the core presenting team on BBC Radio 4's award-winning The Food Programme now in its 40th year, Leyla is also a regular judge for the prestigious annual BBC Food & Farming Awards.

Roman Kemp is one of the country's youngest and most promising broadcasters. Roman has hosted Capital FM's breakfast show for 4 years and has interviewed some of the biggest names in the entertainment industry. Roman made the final of I'm A Celebrity Get Me Out Of Here in 2019, and in 2020 he began hosting 'Sunday Best' on ITV with his dad, Martin which is back in 2021 as 'Weekend Best'.

As well as this, they have appeared in Celebrity Gogglebox for the last two seasons. Earlier this year, Roman fronted his own BBC One documentary, Roman Kemp: Our Silent Emergency, a very raw film around male suicide and mental health.

CEO at British Beauty Council and Director at Brandstand Communications. During her career as a retail maven and brand creator Millie Kendall has been instrumental in the success of cult brands including Shu Uemura, Aveda, Tweezerman and L'Occitane.

In 1997 she founded and created makeup brand, Ruby & Millie cosmetics and was awarded an MBE in 2007 for services to the cosmetics industry. In 2018 she co-founded the British Beauty Council, a non-profit organisation that aims to support a successful, innovative, and inclusive British beauty industry.

Ferdinand Kingsley is a British actor, best known for portraying Charles Elmé Francatelli in ITV's drama series Victoria. His other TV credits include Tom Fontana's Borgia, The Hollow Crown, Ripper Street, Still Star-Crossed, Doctor Who, and Poirot. Ferdinand's film credits include The Last Legion, Van Gogh: Painted With Words, BBC's The Whale and Gary Shore's Dracula Untold.

Ferdinand's theatrical credits include Nicholas Hytner's Hamlet and Simon Godwin's Man And Superman with Ralph Fiennes, both at the National Theatre.

Ferdinand can currently be seen in David Fincher's latest film Mank.

Mark Krendel

Founder, 8lbs

Mark Krendel. Founder, 8lbs. Mark has over a decade's experience structuring innovative deals across the entertainment industry. Having established the digital and commercial divisions at Universal, he founded partnership specialists 8lbs to help talent, rights holders and brands work together.

In addition to delivering campaigns for the likes of Annabel's, boohoo and Xperia, the team is increasingly forging new ways for talent and investors to launch new ventures.

Caspar Lee

YouTuber & entrepreneur

Caspar Lee is a British-South African creator, entrepreneur and investor who rose to prominence with his popular YouTube channel. He's collaborated with many of the world's biggest stars including Ed Sheeran, Dwayne Johnson, Chris Pratt, Kevin Hart and Anna Kendricks. After finding success as an entertainer, Caspar co-founded Influencer.com and took the role of Chief Visionary Officer. The company operates globally with over 70 employees and boasts many of the world's leading brands as clients. Later he co-founded Margravine Management with Joe Sugg. IMG invested and is a strategic partner to the company.

SG Lewis

Singer-songwriter, musician & record producer

SG Lewis' DEBUT album 'times', is fuelled by the longstanding love of disco and created with a renewed focus on SG as a performer and artist as well as producer. The single 'Chemicals' is a soaring, funk- driven track entirely performed and sung by SG himself. SG then released his second single 'Impact' which features Robyn & Channel Tres, later followed by Feed The Fire with Lucky Daye and then One More with the legendary Nile Rodgers. SG has previously collaborated with Col3trane, Raye, Ray BLK, The Neptunes / N.E.R.D's Chad Hugo, Gerd Janson, Conducta and more as well as producing 'Hallucinate' on Dua Lipa's 'Future Nostalgia'.

Hannah Marshall

Creative director & multi-disciplinary artist

HANNAH MARSHALL STUDIO creates immersive art installations and sensory experiences to amplify human connection, individually + collectively. An award—winning British artist notable for her distinct aesthetic of black + light, Marshall is a quiet force who cuts through the noise. Employing minimalism as a visceral agent to distill and connect with raw emotion. Commissioned internationally, the studio creates compelling experiences for conscious and culturally important global brands, artists and spaces to elevate and enforce a message. Clients include; London Borough of Culture, The Science Museum, The British Museum, The Royal Academy of Arts, Nike, Selfridges, Mercedes-Benz and Sony.

Liz Matthews

Entertainment publicist

Liz launched her namesake agency LMPR in 2005 before co-founding Good Culture in 2021, whose mission is to drive ROI for clients by delivering culturally impactful programmes that deliver high levels of engagement. Purpose, responsibility, inclusion and representation are the core values. Over the last decade she has built the careers of the likes of Alexa Chung and Rosie Huntington-Whiteley.

Liz brokered the deal between Pat McGrath Labs and Star Wars; In 2020 Liz worked with Grazia International and Kim Kardashian-West to create a global takeover featuring over 10 International editions.

Zara McDermott

Model & influencer

Zara McDermott is a campaigner, presenter and influencer with 1.5 m followers. She began her career as a civil servant, and was propelled into the spotlight in 2018 after appearing on ITV's 'Love Island'. In 2020 Zara worked with BBC3 to produce a documentary about the controversies surrounding revenge porn and the distribution of non-consensual images. The show was watched by over 6 million people and prompted the BBC to commission another documentary with Zara. She is a supporter for Refuge, fronting their "The Naked Threat" initiative and has recently campaigned in Parliament for a change in the laws around revenge porn.

Natalie Melton

Creative director, The Craft Council

As creative director at the Crafts Council, the UK' national charity for craft, Natalie's role encompasses creative programming for the gallery in London, the publication of Crafts magazine, the leading print authority on craft, and brand, marketing and communications.

From 2012- 2018 she was co-founder and managing director of The New Craftsmen, a business which curates, commissions and sells unique contemporary objects rooted in craftsmanship and narrative made by makers from across the British Isles.

She is a regular spokesperson and commentator on craft in the media.

Nachson Mimran

Founder To.org & Together Band

Nachson Mimran is a father, entrepreneur, co-founder and CEO of to.org, Creative Director and Chairman of the Board of The Alpina Gstaad, and Provocateur in Chief of several organisations including Extreme E.

Founded in 2015 by Nachson and his brother Arieh Mimran, to.org is a venture fund, foundation, and collection of creative endeavours, all focused on accelerating Earth's most vital ventures. With a passion for nature and humanity stemming from a childhood spent in West Africa and Europe, Nachson leverages his network to address Earth's most pressing challenges and ensure the future health of people and planet.

Mr JWW

Co-founder of @ theproductionbunker

Content creator, presenter, racing driver and entrepreneur, MrJWW started his YouTube journey in 2015 with no audience and just an iPhone for a video camera.

His channel has since attracted 130 million views and a global audience of over 1.5 million leading to partnerships and advisory positions with some of the largest brands in the automotive world such as Maserati, Michelin and Aston Martin.

Brenock O'Connor

Actor

Born in 2000, British actor Brenock O'Connor is perhaps best known for his role of 'Olly' in Game of Thrones. Brenock has just wrapped on the second series of Amazon's critically acclaimed television adaptation of Anthony Horowitz' hit series Alex Rider, playing Alex's best friend and sidekick, 'Tom'. Other television work includes Sky's series Living the Dream as 'Freddie', 'Jon' in Channel 4's BAFTA nominated Irish comedy Derry Girls, and BBC series' Dickensian and The Split.

In 2019, Brenock starred as the leading role 'Conor' in the new musical adaptation of hit film Sing Street, which opened at the New York Theatre Workshop.

Dermot O'Leary

Presenter & radio DJ

Dermot O'Leary's is a household name, most notably as the host of ITV's The X Factor. You can now catch Dermot on the This Morning sofa alongside Alison Hammond as a regular host on a Friday morning, discussing the latest topics with the nation in their usual fun style. Off-screen, Dermot is also a successful author of the 'Toto the Ninja Cat' children's book series as well as having the pleasure of hosting UNICEF's Soccer Aid since 2010.

He runs a variety of projects including his weekend Radio 2 show, 'Saturday Breakfast with Dermot O'Leary', his podcast series 'People Are Just People' and a TV show for the BBC titled 'Reel Stories'.

Melissa Odabash

Fashion designer

Highly regarded as the pioneer of luxury swimwear, Melissa Odabash MBE was tipped early on by Vogue as the "Ferraris of Swimwear." Having had a successful career as a model, Melissa Odabash created her own line of swimwear, selling them initially to boutiques in Milan but swiftly gaining global recognition when her designs featured on the covers of American fashion magazines. She continues to have a loyal celebrity following with her designs being worn by A-listers such as Beyoncé, Kate Moss, Sienna Miller, Rihanna, and the Duchess of Cambridge.

Michelle Ogundehin

Writer, consultant & TV presenter

Michelle Ogundehin is a thought leader on interiors, trends, style and wellbeing. Originally trained as an architect and the former Editor-in-Chief of ELLE Decoration UK, she is a regular contributor to publications worldwide including Vogue Living, FT How to Spend It magazine and Dezeen. She is also the Head Judge on BBC1's Interior Design Masters, now filming its third series. Her first book, Happy Inside: How to Harness the Power of Home for Health and Happiness is a one-stop guide to living well — a game-changing look at why your environment is as fundamental to becoming your best self as nutrition and exercise.

Caroline Rush

CEO, British Fashion Council

Since her appointment as Chief Executive in April 2009, Caroline has focused on strengthening the British Fashion Council's network and platforms to connect businesses with global audiences both trade and consumer.

During this time London Fashion Week has become a globally recognised platform for creativite fashion talent, London Fashion Week Men's was launched in 2012 and more recently the four fashion weeks in London have become gender neutral with a pivot to digital for June 2020 and beyond. The Fashion Awards has become the global awards for the fashion industry and has raised £ms for the BFC's charitable projects.

Juliet Sear

TV baker & author

Juliet Sear is one of the UK's leading cakeologists; building a reputation for creativity, innovation and making impressive and challenging cakes accessible to the average baker. Her no-nonsense, down to earth approach makes her creations accessible as well as highly entertaining. Juliet fronted her debut baking show for ITV 'Beautiful Baking With Juliet Sear'.

She is a regular presenter on ITV's This Morning show and designed and created the edible animated characters for Channel 4's Great British Bake Off for their TV, social and print media advertising campaigns.

Niomi Smart

Wellness & lifestyle blogger

Niomi Smart is the founder of vegan and natural skincare brand, Smart Skin and author of best-selling plant-based recipe book, 'Eat Smart'. Niomi has a global audience of more than 4.6 million people. Her digital platforms are the perfect one-stop for wellbeing and self-love. As an Ambassador for the Charity 'Women for Women International' she is proud to support their initiatives to empower women in conflict zones and bring their work to the forefront. She is also the founder of 'Smart Swap', a successful clothes swap event. Niomi was the UK face of L'Oréal Botanicals, the all-natural, vegan haircare brand and is the creator of the L'Occitane lipstick, Sweet Rosé.

James Stewart

Heart Radio host

James has presenting experience across Radio, TV & Social; he hosts Early Breakfast show in the UK, on Heart FM Monday to Friday, and combines this with on-screen red-carpet hosting roles on E! UK, GQ Men Of The Year and Disney UK.

James spent 4 years studying Geography & climate change at The University of Bristol, and speaks with a passion and authority around the subject, as demonstrated by his recent work with the charity WWF.

The Thinking Drinkers

Drinks writers & comedy performers

Tom Sandham & Ben McFarland, aka 'The Thinking Drinkers', are award-winning alcohol experts, authors and comedians.

They write regularly for an array of newspapers and have authored several books on drink – the latest being "The Thinking Drinkers' Almanac".

Having debuted in 2011 at the Edinburgh Fringe Festival, the Thinking Drinkers' shows are now a highlight of the event and they spread their "Drink Less, Drink Better" mantra nationwide, reaching more than 15000 people every year. They are due to return to UK theatres this year with their latest show "Thinking Drinkers Pub Quiz".

John Vial

Celebrity hairdresser & founder, Sloane Salon

John Vial is a globally renowned stylist whose vision, technique and creative flair assures he is constantly in demand from designers, celebrities, magazines and international beauty brands.

He is an industry pacesetter who continues to push creative boundaries. He is the resident Hair Stylist on TV Series 10 Years Younger and is of course is celebrity stylist of choice to a host of leading names from the Spice Girls to Bjork. Collaborations range from Zaha Hadid to Tim Walker.

No one is as passionate about hair as John Vial.

Harriet Vine

MBE creative director & co-founder, Tatty Devine

As Creative Director and Co-founder of Tatty Devine, Harriet is a British artist who constantly pushes the boundaries of what's possible and challenges the very notion of what jewellery design is considered to be. Over twenty years ago, she founded Tatty Devine, the world's go-to brand for original and fun statement jewellery, in East London with her friend Rosie Wolfenden.

Key collaborations include Fawcett Society, Design Museum, Jeremy Deller and Tate. In 2019, Harriet was an expert craft judge on Channel 4's The Fantastical Factory of Curious Craft, has co-authored two books and in 2013, she was awarded an MBE for services to the fashion industry.

Stephen Webster

British jewellery designer

Founded on 40 vibrant years of technical excellence, London based, luxury jewellery designer Stephen Webster, is internationally renowned for his fearless design, traditional craftsmanship, and cutting-edge processes. Rebellious yet ethical, the brand genuinely stands for something good using materials that are always thoughtfully and responsibly sourced, with a commitment to sustainable practices.

With over 100 points of sale worldwide, including the Stephen Webster flagship Mount Street salon, the brand continues to thrive under its Founder and Creative Director, Stephen Webster, and the introduction of Stephen's daughter, Amy Webster.

Sian Welby

TV & radio presenter

Television and radio host Sian Welby can currently be heard every weekday morning on the Capital Breakfast Show that she co-hosts with Roman Kemp and Sonny Jay. They are joined by the biggest guests from the world of entertainment as they wake up the nation from 6am – 10am.

Prior to joining Capital Sian had her own show on Heart where she hosted guests including P!nk, Chris Pratt and Sam Smith, and events like Ed Sheeran's secret live concert to the Regent Street Christmas light's switch-on.

Sian was a weather presenter for Channel 5, where her creative comedy forecasts went viral, racking up 10 million views.

Lucy Williams

Digital creative & consultant

Lucy Williams is a full-time digital creative and brand consultant.

After working in fashion for many years at the likes of Sheerluxe.com, InStyle and trends and innovation advisory Stylus, in 2014 Lucy took her blog full time and has over the last decade built a dedicated global audience and engaged community online.

Lucy now runs three instagram accounts making her platforms an essential destination for effortless, fashion, beauty and travel photography (@lucywilliams02), lifestyle mood boards and inspiration (@remotely) and her newest venture into home and interiors (@lucywilliamshome).

Steven Wilson

Artist

Bonnie Wright

Actress, film-maker & activist

Steven Wilson runs his studio from his home in Brighton, where he creates his varied and experimental work. His Illustrations and typography have been commissioned by clients such as BBH, AKQA, Nike, Virgin, Neiman Marcus, MTV, NYC&GO, AIGA, The Oscars, The New Yorker, Wallpaper Magazine, Sony BMG, Warner Music, Wired and the New York Times.

In the past he's exhibited his work at BBH London, Team One LA and Karl Lagerfeld in London, while he has recently had three exhibitions in Korea, including one at Kumho Museum of Art.

Bonnie Wright is a British actress, best known for her role of Ginny Weasley in all eight of the Harry Potter films.

Bonnie now works behind the camera - directing shorts, commercials and music videos, with projects having premiered at Cannes and Tribeca Film Festival.

Bonnie is a leading climate activist serving as an ambassador for both Greenpeace and Rainforest Alliance. Bonnie's mission is to promote a sustainable lifestyle that can be obtainable and fun.

She is committed to using her social media platforms to further her own education around climate and humanitarian issues.

Charlotte Posner

C H A R L O T T E P O S N E R

Charlotte Posner — cover artist

"All I have ever wanted to do is paint and draw, it's as natural to me as breathing"

Charlotte Posner is a new breed of artistic talent, driven by a passionate need to create art as expression. Her style and popularity exploded onto the public scene in 2014 when she received her first Royal Academy placement as part of the RA summer exhibition and was profiled on BBC TV Culture Show. A Social media frenzy then erupted when she first introduced her 'Pop Dolls' series to the public in 2015. Despite her severe dyslexia, Charlotte's undaunting creative approach shows extraordinary versatility. No ordinary artist, Charlotte has now collaborated with some of the world's leading luxury brands and retailers and has developed collections of gifts to sit alongside her art.

charlotteposner.com

Qualifiying CoolBrands® 2021/22

& Other Stories
1Rebel
67 Pall Mall
Abel & Cole
Acne Studios
Acqua di Parma
Activision Blizzard
adidas
AER Electric
Aēsop
aeydē
Affordable Art Fair
AGA
Agent Provocateur
Air & Grace
Airbnb
Alara
Alessi
Alex Monroe
Alexander McQueen
Alexander Wang
Alighieri
All Points East
Allbirds
AllBright
allplants
Alo
Annina Vogel
Apple
Apple County Cider Co.
Apple TV+
Aprilia
Aram
Arket
Aromatherapy Associates
Artist Residence Hotels
Aspall Cyder
Aston Martin
Astrid & Miyu
ATP Atelier
Audi
Audible
Audio-Technica

Aveda
Avegant
Aviation
AWAY THAT DAY
B&B Italia
Balcones
Balenciaga
Bamford
Bang & Olufsen
Barbican
Barbour
bareMinerals
BBC iPlayer
Beats by Dr. Dre
Beauty Pie
Beautystack
Beavertown
BECCA
BELAZU
Belsazar
Belvedere Vodka
Ben & Jerry's
Bennett Winch
Bentley
Berners Tavern
Berry Bros. & Rudd
Bert & May
Beyond Meat
Beyond Yoga
BFI PLAYER
Bignose & Beardy
Biona Organic
Bird & Blend Tea Co.
Black Cow
Black Eyewear
Black Sheep Brewery
Black Tomato
Blacks Club
Blakes London
Bleach London
BLOK
Bloomsbury
Bloomtown

Boardmasters
Bobbi Brown
Bocca di Lupo
Bodyism
Bollinger
Booja-Booja
Bookshop.org
Bose
Botanic Lab
Bottega Veneta
BOTTLETOP
Bower Collective
Bowers & Wilkins
Brat
Brew Tea Co
Briogeo
British Colour Standard
Brompton
Bugatti
Bulleit
Burberry
Busaba
by CHLOE.
Byredo
Camden Town Brewery
Camp Bestival
CAMPARI
Cannondale
CanO Water
Canon
Caran D'Ache
Caravan
Carpano
Cartier
Casamigos
Casely-Hayford
Cass Art
Caterham
Celine
CHANEL
Chantecaille
Chapel Down
Charbonnel et Walker

Charlotte Mensah
Charlotte Tilbury
Chartreuse
Chase Distillery
Chilly's
Christopher Kane
Church's
Citymapper
Clase Azul
Coco de Mer
Codecademy
Coldpress
Comme des Garçons
Compass Box
Condé Nast College
Conscious Chocolate
Converse All Stars
Coppa Club
Core
Cornerstone
COS
Cowshed
Craft Gin Club
Craig Green
Crystal Head Vodka
CUBE
Cubitt
Cult Beauty
Curious Brewery
Curve
Curzon
Cutler and Gross
Daisy
Darjeeling Express
Dark Star Brewing Co.
Dash Water
Daylesford
De'Longhi
Dermalogica
Dior
diptyque
Discarded Spirits
Dishoom

Doisy & Dam
Dollar Shave Club
Dom Pérignon
Don Julio
Dorset Cereals
Dorset Nectar
Dover Street Market
Dr Sebagh
Dr Stuart's
Dr. Hauschka
Dr. Jackson's
Dr. Martens
Dr. Vranjes
DreamWorks
Dries Van Noten
Drunk Elephant
Dualit
Ducati
DuckDuckGo
Dunkertons
Duolingo
Dyson
E.C. One
Earl of East
East London Liquor Company
Eco Bath London
Ecosia
Ecover
Edward Green
Electric Cinema
Electronic Arts (EA)
Elephant Gin
Empirical
EMS
END.
Enigma
Epic Games
Erbology
ercol
Erdem
Etsy
Everyman Cinemas
Eyeko
Faber & Faber
Faber-Castell
FAIR.
FALKE

Farfetch
Farmdrop
Farrow & Ball
Fender Play
Fentimans
Fenty Beauty & Fenty Skin
Ferrari
Fever-Tree
Fierce Grace
Finisterre
Fired Earth
first direct
Fitbit
Five Guys
Fjällräven Kånken
Flat Iron
Flight Club
Flos
FOREO
Fortnum & Mason
Four Pillars
Fourpure Brewing Company
Foyles
Frame
Franco Manca
Frieze London
fritz-kola
Gaggenau
GAIL'S
Garmin
ghd
Gingerline
Glastonbury
Glossier
GO Kombucha
Gocycle
Good & Proper Tea
Google
GoPro
Gosnells of London
Graham & Brown
Graham and Green
Green Man Festival
Grenson
GREY GOOSE
Grind
GUBI

Gucci
Gymshark
Haeckels
Haig Club
Ham Yard Hotel
Hanro
Harman Kardon
Harry's
Hasselblad
Hattingley Valley
Hauser & Wirth
Hawkes
Hawksmoor
HAY
Heal's
Hedonism Wines
Heist
Heliocare
Hendrick's Gin
Herbivore
Hernö Gin
Herradura
Herschel Supply Co
Hershesons
Hibiki
Hillier Bartley
HINE
Hive
Home Grown
Homeslice
Honest
Honest Grapes
HonestBrew
Hotpod Yoga
Hourglass
House of Hackney
Huda Beauty
Hunter
ICONIC London
iderma
IKEA
Illamasqua
Instagram
Institute of Contemporary Arts
Isabel Marant
Isle of Wight Festival
itsu

J.W. Anderson
Jacquemus
Jaguar
James Read
Jasper Morrison
Jax Coco
Jil Sanders
Jo Malone
Joe & Seph's
Joe's Tea Co.
Johnnie Walker
Joseph Cheaney & Sons
Jude's
Junkyard Golf Club
Kallø
Karma Drinks
KeepCup
Ketel One Botanical
KETTLE Chips
KEVIN.MURPHY
Kiehl's
Kiln
Kin
Kindle
Kip
Kirk & Kirk
Kiss the Moon
KitchenAid
Kitri
Klarna
Knoll
KTM
KX
La Perla
Laphroaig
L'Artisan Parfumeur
Laura Mercier
Laurent-Perrier
Le Creuset
Legendary Pictures
Leica
Leiths School of Food and Wine
Leon
Liberty
Lick
Liforme
Ligne Roset

Lime Wood
Linda Farrow
Little Greene
Living Architecture
Living Proof
Lizi's Granola
Lo Bros
Loake
Loewe
Lomography
London Art Fair
London Essence Company
London Fields Brewery
lookfantastic
Lovebox
LoveRaw
Ludlow Food Festival
Lululemon
Lusso Stone
M·A·C
Made
Maison Margiela
MALIN+GOETZ
Mallow & Marsh
MAMONT vodka
Manolo Blahnik
Manomasa
Maria Black
Maria Tash
Marvel Studios
MasterClass
MATCHESFASHION.COM
Matilda Goad
McLaren
MEATliquor
Melissa Odabash
MelodyVR
Mercedes-Benz
method
Miele
Milk Makeup
Mindful Chef
MINI
Missoma
Mixcloud
MOA Magic Organic Apothecary
Modibody

Moleskine
Molly Goddard
Molteni&C
Moneybox
Monica Vinader
Monkey Shoulder
Monmouth Coffee Company
Monzo
Moroccanoil
Mr & Mrs Smith
Mr Lyan's
Mr Organic
MR PORTER
MUBI
Mulberry
Munchy Seeds
Nails.INC
Naked Wines
NARS
Native
Natural History Museum
NatureLab
Neal's Yard Remedies
Neom Organics
Neous
NET-A-PORTER.COM
Netflix
New Balance
Nicholas Kirkwood
Nike
NIKKA Whisky
Nikon
Nintendo
Nkuku
Nobu Hotels
Nom
Non Plastic Beach
Northern Bloc
Northern Monk
Nota Bene
Nubian Skin
Nutmeg
Nutribullet
Nyetimber
OceanSaver
Oculus
OFF-WHITE

OLAPLEX
Old Mout Cider
Ole & Steen
Oliver Peoples
Oliver Spencer
Olivia von Halle
Olympus
Ombar
onefinestay
Opening Ceremony
OPI
Oppo
Orchard Pig
Oribe
Orlebar Brown
Osborne & Little
OSKIA
Ottolenghi
OUAI
Our/Vodka
Oyster Yachts
Pact Coffee
Palace
Paramount Pictures
Parklife
Pashley
Pat McGrath Labs
Patagonia
Patrón Tequila
Patty & Bun
Paul Ainsworth at No6
Peloton
Penguin
Perky Blenders
Perrier
Perrier-Jouët
Persol
Phine
Picturehouse Cinemas
Pinterest
Pizza Pilgrims
Planet Organic
PlayStation
Plenish
Plymouth Gin
Pol Roger
Polaroid

Pollen + Grace
Polly's Brew Co.
Pooky
Porsche
Portobello Rd Gin
POSCA
Prada
Pressure Drop Brewing
Prestat
Primrose's Kitchen
PROPERCORN
Psycle
Pukka
Pump Street Chocolate
Punchdrunk
Purdey's
Pureology
RA (Royal Academy)
Random House
Rapanui
Rapha
Rare Tea Company
Raw Halo
Ray Stitch
Ray-Ban
REAL Kombucha
Rebel Kitchen
Reddit
Remeo Gelato
REN Clean Skincare
Republic of Fritz Hansen
RevitaLash Cosmetics
Revolut
Reyka Vodka
Richard Quinn
RICOH THETA
Ridgeview
RIEDEL
Ring
River Cottage Cookery School
Riverford
Rock Rose
Rockett St George
Rockstar Games
Rococo Chocolates
Roksanda
Rosewood London

ROWBOTS
Roxanne First
Royal Enfield
Rude Health
Ruinart
Rustler Yachts
S.Pellegrino
Sacai
Saint Laurent
Samsung
Sand & Sky
Sandqvist
Savage X Fenty
SCP
Sea Containers London
Secret Cinema
Seed & Bean
Seedlip
SEGA
Segway-Ninebot
Self Care Co.
Selfridges
Sennheiser
Sharpham Park
Shaun Leane
Shazam
Shiseido
Shoreditch House
Shoryu Ramen
Simone Rocha
Sipsmith
Siren Craft Brew
Skandium
SK-II
SkinCeuticals
Smeg
Soho House
Sol de Janeiro
Sonos
Sony
Sophia Webster
SoulCycle
SoundCloud
Southbank Centre
Space NK
Specialized
Spectrum

Spotify
SQUARE ENIX
Squirrel Sisters
Starling Bank
Stella McCartney
Stephen Webster
St-Germain
Stitch & Story
Strathmore
Street Feast Festival
Sunseeker
Superga
Symprove
Taittinger
TALA
Tangle Teezer
Tapatio
TÅPPED
Tate
Tatty Devine
teapigs
TED
Ten Health & Fitness
TENZING
Tequila Fortaleza
Tequila Ocho
Tesla
The Arts Club
The Beauty Chef
The Botanist
The Connaught
The Five Points Brewing Co
The Fordwich Arms
The Forest Side
The Groucho Club
The Hand & Flowers
The Handmade Cocktail Company
The Hepworth Wakefield
The House of St Barnabas
The Hoxton
The Isle Of Paradise
The Ivy Club
The Kernel Brewery
The London EDITION
The Lowry Hotel
The Natural Deodorant Co.
The New Craftsmen

The North Face
The Nue Co.
The Ordinary
THE OUTNET
The Paleo Food Co
The Palomar
The Pig
The Raw Chocolate Company
The River Café
The Rookery
The Rug Company
The Sportsman, Seasalter
The Standard, London
The Third Space
The V&A
The Vampire's Wife
The Wild Beer Co
The Zetter Townhouses
This Works
TikTok
tokyobike
Tom Dixon
TOM FORD
TOMS
Tonkotsu
Tony's Chocolonely
Trafalger Studios
Trek
Tricker's
TriPollar
Triumph
triyoga
TRNSMT
Twitch
Tyrrells
Ubisoft
Unbound
Under Armour
Universal Music Group
Universal Pictures
Vagabond Coffee Roasters
VanMoof
Vans
Veja
Verdant Brewing Co.
Vespa
Vetements

Veuve Clicquot
Vintage Electric
Vita Coco
Vitamix
Vitra
Vivobarefoot
VOSS
Wahl
WallpaperSTORE*
Walt Disney
Warner Bros.
Warner Music Group
WaterRower
Waze
Wealthify
WelleCo
WhatsApp
Wheely
Wheyhey
Whitechapel Gallery
Whole Earth
Whole Foods Market
Widow Jane
Wild
Wild Card Brewery
Wilderness
Wildsmith Skin
Willie's Cacao
Winsor & Newton
Wireless Festival
Wolf & Badger
Wolford
Wool and the Gang
Xbox
Yallah
Yodomo
YOGI TEA
YouTube
YSP (Yorkshire Sculpture Park)
Zanzan
Zipcar
Zoom
Żubrówka